Deserts

CONTENTS

© Aladdin Books Ltd 1986

Designed and produced by
Aladdin Books Ltd
70 Old Compton Street
London W1

First published in the
United States in 1987 by
Gloucester Press
387 Park Avenue South
New York NY 10016

Printed in Belgium

ISBN 0-531-17037-3

Library of Congress Catalog
Card Number: 86-82810

Certain illustrations have previously appeared in the "Closer Look"
series published by Gloucester Press.

The consultant on this book, JL Cloudsley-Thompson,
is Professor of Zoology, Birkbeck College,
University of London, UK.

A CLOSER LOOK AT

Deserts

JILL HUGHES

Illustrated by

ROY COOMBS AND MAURICE WILSON

Consultant

J.L. CLOUDSLEY-THOMPSON

Gloucester Press
New York · Toronto · 1987

The desert

Most people imagine a desert as a vast, sandy waste like the Sahara, in north Africa, or the sands of Arabia. Sand dunes stretch as far as the eye can see and the only travelers are the camel caravans.

Different deserts

In fact any area where the rainfall is less than 25 cm (9.8 in) a year is called a desert. There are "cold deserts" in the Arctic and Antarctic. In this book, however, we will be finding out about hot deserts. Here the dryness and the extreme temperatures – very hot in the day and cold at night – make life difficult. But some plants, animals and human beings are able to survive in such conditions. Modern technology has helped man to survive and master the desert, but for centuries people have known ways of living in harmony with it.

A Bedouin Arab leads his camel, loaded with firewood, through an oilfield. Here the traditional life of the desert contrasts with modern man's attempts to get at the hidden wealth beneath the desert sands.

Deserts of the world

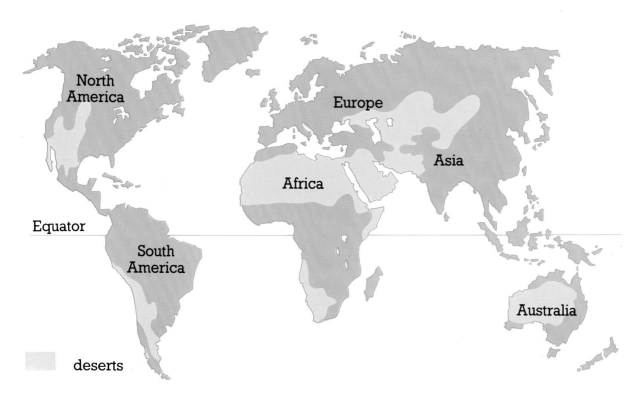

North America

Europe

Asia

Africa

Equator

South America

Australia

deserts

Hot deserts are found in two belts stretching right around the world above and below the Equator. In the Northern Hemisphere there are deserts in Africa (the Sahara), Arabia, Central Asia (the Gobi) and North America. In the Southern Hemisphere there are deserts in southern Africa (the Kalahari), Australia and South America. The Gobi desert has cold winters and the stony ground grows thin grass. The Australian desert is a land of red earth covered by low-growing scrub.

The map shows the main areas of desert in the world. Only the Gobi desert, high up in Central Asia, and the high Atacama desert in Peru have cold winters.

Desert conditions

All deserts have one thing in common – their dryness. Rain may not fall for years and when it does, it quickly vanishes into the parched ground.

1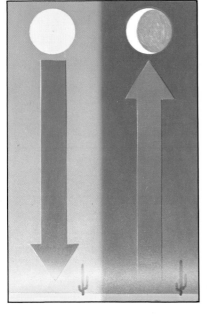

2

(1) In the day, when the sun is at its height, the deserts bake. At night, heat quickly escapes from the cooling ground.

(2) In a tropical forest, rain clouds prevent the daytime temperature from getting too high. At night the clouds help to keep the heat in.

Heat and dryness

Most of the world's deserts are situated at roughly the same distance from the Equator, north or south. They lie in very warm regions near the Tropic of Cancer (north of the Equator) and the Tropic of Capricorn (south of the Equator). We usually think of the tropics as being "steamy" and wet – and so they are, where there are rain forests and mountains and rain clouds.

There are a few clouds over deserts, but it seldom rains. This is because most deserts lie in a "rain shadow," on the leeward or sheltered side of a mountain range. Warm, moisture-laden winds from the oceans hit the windward side of the range. There they are cooled and consequently drop their rain. When they reach the other side and pass over the desert, these winds have lost all their moisture so no rain falls.

How deserts are made

This archway of sandstone in a North American desert was carved by the action of wind.

We have seen that deserts exist where there is very little rain. But *how* do deserts take the forms they do? The landscapes of deserts have been formed over many thousands of years by natural forces, such as the wind and rain, acting on the rocks and soils of a particular region.

Wind and water power

The two strongest forces involved in creating deserts are wind and water. Winds blow hard over land where no trees break their force, moving earth, rocks and sand. Torrential rain and rivers cut deep into the earth.

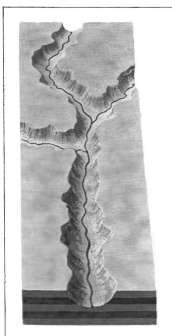

These pictures show three stages in the making of a desert landscape by water. First, rivers flow across a wide plain.

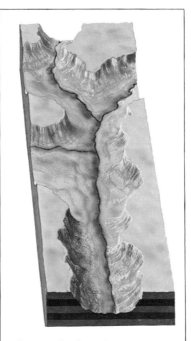

Second, the river, over a process that takes thousands of years, cuts deeper and deeper into the land, creating steep-sided canyons.

Third, the original river bed creates a new plain. A few rocks which have resisted the pressure of water tower above the land.

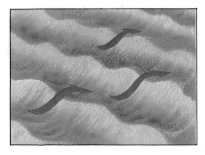

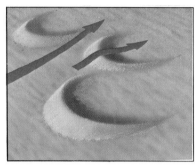
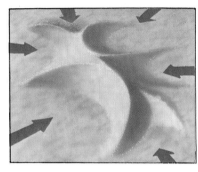

In sandy deserts the wind blows the sand into dunes. The different shapes of the dunes are the result of the direction in which the wind blows.

Where the wind blows

The winds that blow over deserts are dry and strong. They carry with them fragments of rock and grains of sand which act like sandpaper on any surface they hit, wearing away solid rock. In the sandstone deserts of the southwestern United States they carve out strange rock formations.

Topsoil needs plants to anchor it to the ground but the wind uproots the plants and blows away the fertile soil leaving bare rock. This process is called "erosion."

Rushing water

When rain does fall on deserts it usually comes as a sudden thunderstorm creating raging torrents. These form rivers which eventually carve out deep gullies in the dry land. This is how the Grand Canyon, 1.6 km (1 mile) deep, was formed in North America.

Water of life

All living things, plants and animals, need water to live and grow. In deserts life often has to depend on very scarce rainfall, on dew or underground sources of water. When it does rain, it is usually a short, sharp shower. Much of the water just runs off the dry ground or evaporates in the heat of the sun. However, some is held between layers of underground rock. In places this underground water is forced to the surface. Then a fertile area, called an oasis, is created where plants can grow.

Plants play their part

Elsewhere in the dry desert plants manage to trap dew in the early morning. Others have extremely long roots to reach underground water supplies. Plants must flourish because, as the diagram opposite illustrates, they are vital to every other form of life.

Sudden rainstorms often cause "flash" floods in the desert. The ground cannot absorb all the water and raging torrents flood the flat ground and sweep away soil and vegetation.

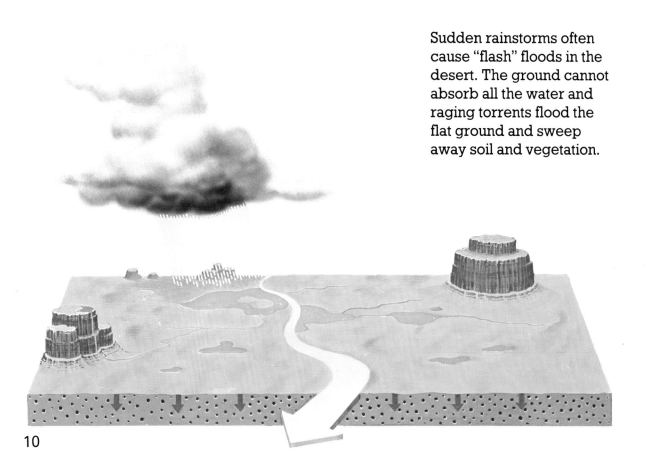

Living things in the desert, as everywhere else on Earth, are linked together by "food-chains." The diagram illustrates how the food chain can be split up into three strands, or separate chains, and how they are connected. In sunlight plants use water and carbon dioxide from the air to make food. The plants in their turn are food for insects, birds and mammals. Some animals feed directly on plants. Others are part of more elaborate chains: insects eat plants; reptiles eat insects; birds and small mammals eat the reptiles and are themselves eaten by larger mammals. All plants and animals die and decay – are broken down by bacteria – and return to the earth to enrich the soil.

Waiting for water

Plants need water not just to live but to produce seeds. Desert plants have a number of ways of coping with their dry home. Many seeds survive for years, apparently dead but really just waiting for the first rainfall to force them into life. The seeds have tough outer skins to protect them.

Plants in a hurry

Once the seeds split their skins and send out shoots into the newly damp earth, the plants grow at a tremendous rate. They flower and produce new seeds in a few weeks. Suddenly the desert is a carpet of brilliant color. When the flowers die, new seeds are left behind on the desert floor to await the next rain.

Sturt's pea is one of the plants whose seeds are protected by a chemical coat that will only dissolve if there is enough rain to ensure the shoot will develop and flower.

This poppy completes its whole life cycle from shoot to plant with buds, and from flower to fruit and new seeds in just a few days.

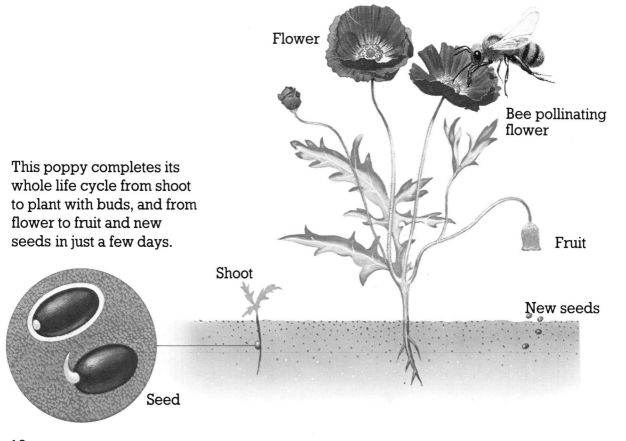

Flower

Bee pollinating flower

Fruit

Shoot

New seeds

Seed

Insects hatch from their eggs when the rain comes. Desert plants have such short lives that they need to attract insects quickly to pollinate their flowers. This is why so many of them are brightly colored.

Carpet of snow

Mexican poppy

Cleome

Fan flower

Annual saltbush

Pterigeron

Permanent plants

While some plants live short, fast lives to take advantage of brief rainfalls, others spread out their life cycles over many years. Plants such as the cacti of the American deserts and the baobab trees of Africa store water in their stems or trunks. Their shallow roots are widely spread to catch dew as well as rain. The hollow trunk of a baobab can hold as much as 1,000 liters (220 gals) of water. Other plants send their roots down deep into the water-bearing rock.

Slow-growing giants

Of the 200 or more species of cacti that live in the American deserts, the most impressive is the giant saguaro. This is the tall, many-armed cactus you see in cowboy films! It survives the desert drought by storing water in its fleshy stem. Its cousin the barrel cactus has a pleated stem which expands like an accordion to take in water.

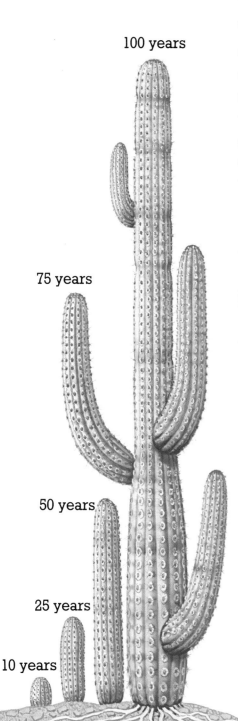

100 years

75 years

50 years

25 years

10 years

The saguaro cactus grows slowly because it gets little water. It can reach a height of 15m (49ft).

Aloe lily

Succulent

Protecting the water store

Many "permanent" plants have thick, waterproof coverings which prevent water escaping and evaporating in the heat. The pores in the plant covering can also be closed to conserve water. The leaves of cactus plants have been replaced by spines or prickles. The spines help to break up air currents around the plant, keeping it in a "jacket" of still air which is less drying. The prickles also protect the plants against animals – any plant which is unpleasant to eat will live longer! The saguaro further guards its water supply by having a powerful poison in its sap to deter tasters.

Surface water

The creosote bush of the United States relies on dew and small amounts of surface water. Its tiny rootlets reach through cracks in the soil. It needs a large area of ground to grow.

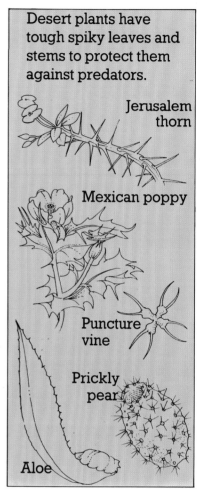

Desert plants have tough spiky leaves and stems to protect them against predators.

Jerusalem thorn

Mexican poppy

Puncture vine

Prickly pear

Aloe

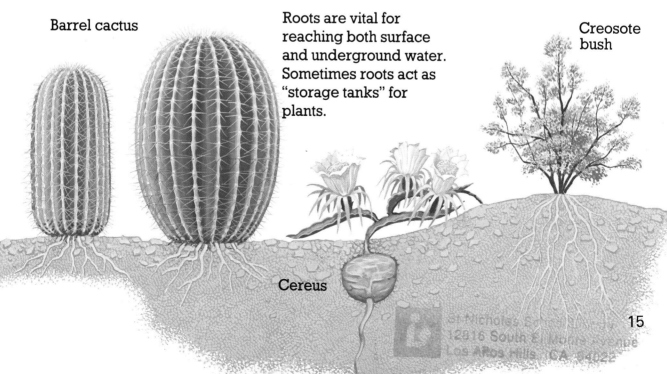

Barrel cactus

Roots are vital for reaching both surface and underground water. Sometimes roots act as "storage tanks" for plants.

Creosote bush

Cereus

The insect population

Insects are the largest animal population in the desert. With their small bodies encased in tough outer shells coated with wax, they need little water , conserving what they have efficiently. They can creep into tiny crevices to shelter from the heat. Their eggs, like the seeds of plants, can survive long periods without water.

Foraging for food

Flying insects like butterflies and moths adapt their lives to suit the brief flowering seasons of the desert. Others, especially beetles, live a semi-underground life, keeping cool and feeding off decaying plant or animal remains in the soil. The darkling beetle of the Namib desert of South Africa comes out at night, when the sea fog rolls over the desert. Drops of water condense on its body. By tilting its body, the beetle can make these drops drain into its mouth.

Darkling beetle

(1) When rain does fall on the desert, plants spring up, insects hatch out and pollinate the flowers – and provide a feast for the desert birds and animals.
(2) As the land dries out, the desert birds and animals eat scattered seeds and insect larvae.

The diagram shows the two types of locusts. Both types can develop from the same sort of egg. Swarming locusts develop at times of over-crowding and take flight in huge swarms, often eating everything in their path. Usually, solitary locusts develop. As their name suggests, these live alone. "Hopper" describes a young locust of either type.

Sahara gecko

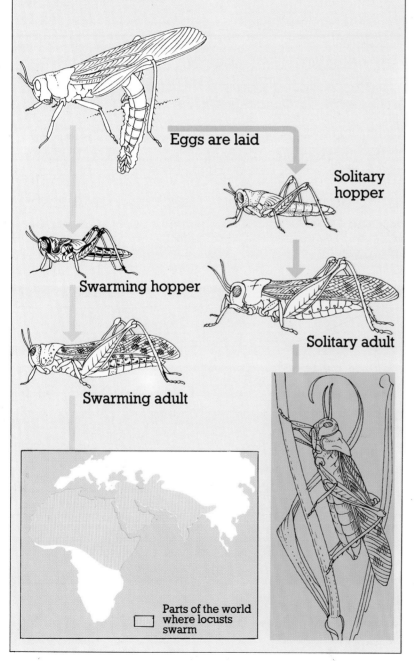

Eggs are laid

Solitary hopper

Swarming hopper

Solitary adult

Swarming adult

Parts of the world where locusts swarm

Hoopoe

Desert hedgehog

The desert animals above benefit from the swarms of locusts. Any type of insect is a good supplement to their diet.

Spiders and scorpions

A scorpion seizes a centipede in its jaws and stings it with its tail.

The long spindly legs and the hard, outer casings of the bodies of spiders and scorpions make them look like insects. In fact they belong to a different animal group called the "arachnids." They have eight legs instead of an insect's six. They live in burrows or under rocks and come out to hunt at night.

Sting in the tail

Scorpions are found in the countries of the southern and eastern Mediterranean as well as in Asia, Africa and the Americas. They eat spiders and insects, seizing their prey with their claws and killing their victims with the sting at the end of their tails. Scorpions can be 10 to 20cm (4 to 8in) long and some species are deadly to human beings.

Below, a stinging wasp catches a tarantula (1) and drags the body back to its burrow (2). There it lays its eggs (3). When these hatch the tarantula provides their first meal (4).

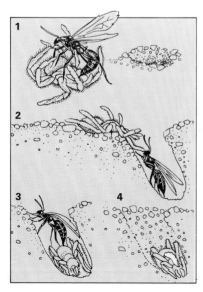

Wolf spider

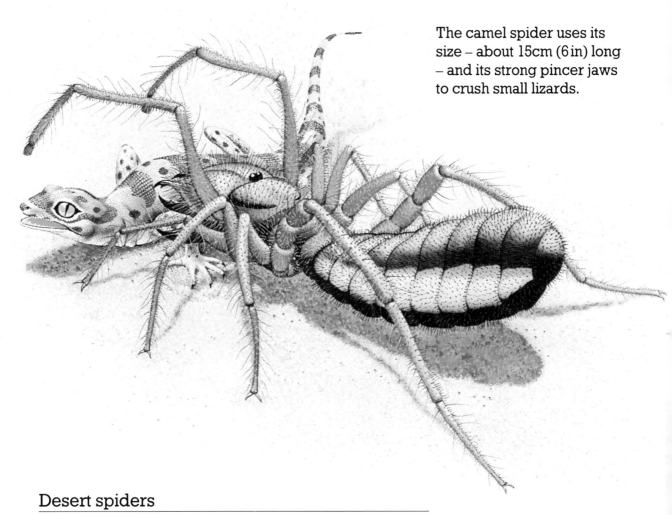

The camel spider uses its size – about 15cm (6 in) long – and its strong pincer jaws to crush small lizards.

Desert spiders

Desert spiders can be large – a tarantula is the size of a man's fist – and all of them look quite fearsome. However, very few are poisonous to, or even bite, humans. Like scorpions they feed on insects by sucking out the body fluids of their victims.

The trapdoor spider, as its name suggests, has a special method of catching prey. It hides in its burrow, covering the entrance with a fine, silky web. When an unsuspecting insect walks on the web, the spider is alerted by the vibrations and seizes it at once. The large, hairy tarantulas and equally fierce but smaller wolf spiders (2.5cm (1in)) have poisonous bites.

19

Reptiles

Warm-blooded animals like birds and mammals keep a constant body temperature. Reptiles, however, are cold-blooded. They need heat from the sun to warm them but they must not allow themselves to get too hot. When it is cold and their body temperatures drop, they become slow and sleepy. If conditions become too cold, they will die.

All kinds of reptiles are found in deserts; for example, snakes, lizards and tortoises. They move about in the few hours after sunset, while the ground is still warm, and after sunrise, before it gets too hot. The scaly skins of reptiles help to prevent water loss.

You would never see all these creatures together at one time, but the picture shows how many different reptiles are found in one desert in Arizona. In the heat of the day most of them burrow under the sand or creep under rocks. When they do move they dart about rapidly to avoid contact with the burning earth.

Keeping cool

One way reptiles can keep cool is to live underground where the temperature is several degrees cooler than on the surface. Some desert animals are shaped to cope with the heat. For example, most desert lizards have long legs so their bodies can avoid contact with the hot sand.

When tortoises get hot they wet their heads and necks with saliva or release water from their bladders over their back legs.

Smooth-moving snakes

Sidewinder snakes of the American deserts and the horned vipers of the Sahara have a unique way of moving over the desert floor. They raise their heads, the center of their bodies and their tails so that they look like bent pins and then shoot the front part of their bodies forward and sideways.

The uses of scales

The smooth scales of snakes allow them to glide through sand without friction. Snakes have a row of broader scales along their undersides which they can use to grip the ground and haul themselves along.

A constrictor is a snake that kills its prey by squeezing it to death.

Poisonous snakes kill by injecting their venom into their prey through teeth called fangs. Boomslangs (1) have fangs at the back of the mouth, rattlesnakes (2) and cobras (3) at the front.

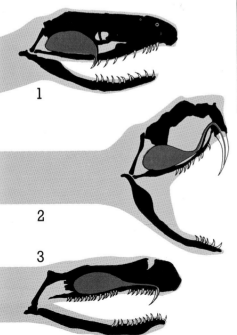

1

2

3

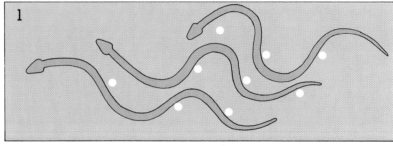

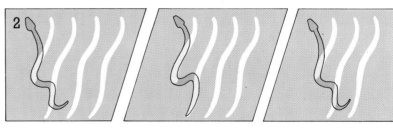

(1) Some snakes use the uneven surface of the ground to loop along like a wave. (2) A sidewinder literally moves sideways.

(3) Vipers move straight forward, gripping the ground with broad scales on their bellies.

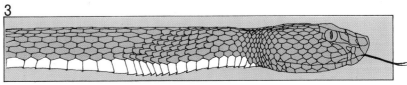

Rattlesnakes live in the discarded burrows of other animals. They use their rattles to warn off foxes or other big animals who may investigate the burrows in search of food.

Rattlesnakes

Rattlesnakes live in the deserts of North and South America. They get their name from the sound they make when they shake their tails, which actually do rattle. The little pits or hollows on either side of their jaws are sensitive to heat and tell them when warm-blooded animals are near. They also have a very keen sense of smell. They have poison fangs and, like all snakes, special jaws which allow them to swallow their prey whole.

A deadly lizard

At sunrise in the western American desert, the Gila monster comes out to hunt. About 30cm (12 in) long, with bright pink and black scales, this lizard can be dangerous! The Gila monster and the beaded lizard of South America are the only poisonous lizards in the world.

The bright colors of the Gila monster signal to larger animals that it is poisonous and that they should not try to attack it.

Desert birds

Birds cope well with desert conditions. Because they can fly, they are free to move about in search of water. Feathers, which keep them warm in cool climates by insulating against the cold, protect them in deserts from the burning sun. If they do get hot they can cool down with the bird's equivalent of panting. They open their beaks and flutter their throats, allowing a current of air to pass across the damp inside of the mouth. Gliding birds escape the heat of the day by allowing air currents to carry them to a cool 900m (3,000ft) above ground.

A quiet life

Flying uses a lot of energy and creates heat so birds tend to stay in one place when they have found a nesting site. Their feathers blend in with the rocks or sand and camouflage them in the dangerous open ground of the desert.

The American roadrunner hunts lizards and snakes on the ground, running rapidly over the desert floor rather than flying. It may run as fast as 40km (25 miles) per hour.

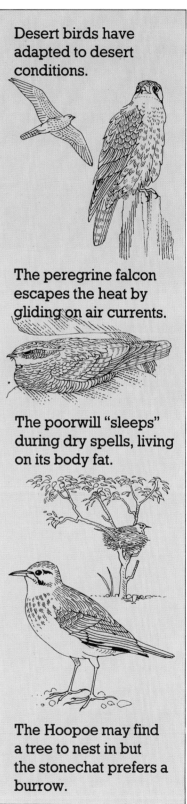

Desert birds have adapted to desert conditions.

The peregrine falcon escapes the heat by gliding on air currents.

The poorwill "sleeps" during dry spells, living on its body fat.

The Hoopoe may find a tree to nest in but the stonechat prefers a burrow.

The American Gila
woodpecker's nest is a
hollow saguaro cactus. The
cactus has to protect its
water supply by growing a
"skin" around the nest hole.

Many desert birds are
gound-living – they walk or
run in search of prey or to
avoid enemies.

Ostrich

Bustard

Rhea

Spur-winged plover

Stone curlew

Courser

Sand grouse

Small mammals

Mammals are warm-blooded animals who feed their young with their own milk. Many of them have fur coats. Most of the desert mammals are small and can shelter in burrows or under rocks in the day out of the heat of the sun.

Tiny, mouselike gerbils and the kangaroo rats stop up the entrances to their burrows. Any moisture they breathe out then gets trapped and can be reused. Desert mammals lead a nocturnal life, kept warm in the cold desert night by their furry coats.

Shaped for heat

Desert animals are thinner than those in cool climates. Their slender frames need less effort to carry about and their long limbs increase the surface area from which cooling can take place. Huge ears, lined with blood vessels, catch any cooling breezes.

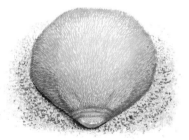

The African golden mole can burrow through sand with its covered eyes.

The Arizona jack rabbit shelters under a cactus from the heat while the kangaroo rat seals itself deep inside a cool burrow.

26

Because of the lack of cloud, the moon sheds a brilliantly clear light over the desert at night. This is when the mammals come out to feed. The gerbil searches for seeds. The hedgehog looks for insects. The fennec fox listens with its huge ears and sniffs with its keen nose, hoping to catch a gerbil.

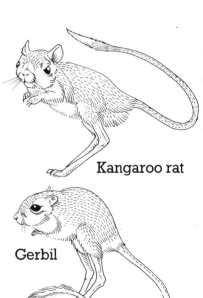

Kangaroo rat

Gerbil

The American kangaroo rat and the Saharan gerbil have both developed long legs for hopping over the desert sand.

Ships of the desert

The largest desert animal is the camel. Its large, flattened feet prevent it from sinking into the sand. In a sandstorm a camel can close its nostrils and its long eyelashes protect its eyes. Furthermore, the camel can travel for long periods without drinking. Its hump contains fat which it can live on for weeks without having to feed.

For centuries the camel was the only form of transport and beast of burden in the desert. These strange and hardy creatures are still vitally important to the survival of desert people like the Bedouin.

There are two kinds of camel: the dromedary has one hump and lives in the Middle East, Africa and India. The two-humped Bactrian camel comes from the cooler deserts of Central Asia. It has a longer coat and shorter legs than the dromedary.

Dorcas gazelle   Addax

Oryx

Gazelles and antelope are among the larger wild animals found in the Sahara. Special efforts have been made in recent years to preserve the shy Arabian oryx from extinction. These large animals can travel over long distances to look for water, or can survive for long periods without drinking.

Wild asses live on the steppes of Central Asia in herds. The nomadic peoples of the region milk the asses and tame them for use as pack animals.

Desert peoples

In all the deserts of the world there have been native peoples who have learned to live in the harsh conditions. Most of them have been nomads – people who travel from place to place. In America there were the Indians, in Australia the Aborigines, the Mongol tribes in Central Asia and the Bushmen of the Kalahari in southern Africa.

Small populations of these people survive today even though modern civilization and its governments prefer to settle people in one place. Among the most successful survivors are the Bedouin tribes of the Middle East and the Arabian peninsula.

The Bedouin

Many Bedouin still lead a traditional life, pitching their dark tents in the desert, herding camels, goats and sheep for a living. They are hospitable people but fiercely independent. In summer they sometimes move to the outskirts of oasis towns but in winter they take to the desert.

Cave paintings found in the Sahara and dating back at least 5,000 years show that it was once a place where great herds of grazing animals roamed and men tended and hunted them.

Part of the traditional life of the Bedouin is hawking. Peregrine falcons are trained to hunt hares or birds. The falcons are carried on the wrist and their hoods removed when game is sighted.

The goat hair or camel hair tents of the Bedouin can be put up in about an hour. In summer heat the poles are raised up vertically and the sides of the tent tied up for coolness. In a sandstorm the poles can be lowered to give less resistance to wind.

Glossary

Altitude The height of land above sea level.

Arachnids Animal group to which the eight-legged spiders and scorpions belong.

Dune A hill or large ridge of sand piled up by the wind.

Erosion What happens when topsoil is washed away by water or blown away by wind.

Evaporation The process in which water turns into water vapor when it is heated.

Flash flood Sudden flood caused by a huge amount of water falling on dry land which cannot absorb it.

Mammal Warm-blooded animal, often with a fur coat, which feeds its young with its own milk.

Nocturnal A nocturnal animal is one which is active at night.

Oasis (plural Oases) A place in the desert where there is water, allowing vegetation to flourish.

Reptile A cold-blooded animal with a scaly skin – snakes, lizards, tortoises and crocodiles are reptiles.

Index